Original title:
Giggles Beneath the Greenwood

Copyright © 2025 Creative Arts Management OÜ
All rights reserved.

Author: Alexander Thornton
ISBN HARDBACK: 978-1-80567-405-4
ISBN PAPERBACK: 978-1-80567-704-8

Rhythms of Radiance in the Foliage

In the shade where shadows play,
Squirrels dance and mice display.
Leaves in laughter loop and spin,
Whispers of joy tucked within.

Frogs in a chorus croak with glee,
Tickling toads join in with spree.
Sunlight flickers in playful beams,
Painting the day with golden dreams.

Breezes tease the branches high,
Chasing secrets through the sky.
Rabbits hop and kittens pounce,
Nature's jesters all announce.

Caterpillars in funny hats,
Make their way on tops of mats.
Every moment, laughter grows,
In this realm of playful shows.

Invitations to Innocent Mischief

Underneath the sprawling trees,
Critters scheme and tease the bees.
Foxes prance with a cheeky grin,
While playful winds begin to spin.

In the meadows, children chase,
Puppies leap with joyful grace.
Butterflies flit in dizzy dives,
As the heart of nature thrives.

Laughter bubbles, oh what fun,
Chasing shadows on the run.
Every rustle brings delight,
As dusk dances into night.

Hiding giggles under cloak,
Echoes of a joyful joke.
In this realm of sweet surrender,
Mischief lingers—never tender.

Whispers of Laughter in the Canopy

Branches sway in playful dance,
Squirrels chatter, take a chance.
Underneath the leafy veil,
Laughter spreads, a joyful trail.

Mushrooms giggle in the dew,
Each petal paints a smile anew.
Sunbeams tickle, shadows prance,
Nature weaves a merry dance.

Secrets of the Sylvan Meadow

Butterflies with painted wings,
Whisper tales that laughter brings.
Flowers wink as breezes sigh,
Hidden joys that flit and fly.

In the thickets, secrets play,
Every sound a child's ballet.
Ticklish grass beneath our feet,
Nature's laughter, soft and sweet.

Joyful Echoes Among the Leaves

Echoes bounce from tree to tree,
Notes of glee in harmony.
A rustle hints at playful feats,
Where hilarity discreetly meets.

Dancing shadows, light as air,
All around, a lively flare.
Chirping birds join in the fun,
Underneath the warming sun.

Chuckles in the Shade of Ancient Trees

Under canopies so grand,
Laughter tumbles through the land.
Old trunks twist with a cheeky grin,
As woodland friends invite us in.

Dandelions share their jokes,
Playing tricks on passing blokes.
Each rustling leaf a merry shout,
In this realm where smiles sprout.

Lively Tales from the Bark and Bramble

In the thicket where the critters play,
Squirrels dance in a cheeky ballet.
Witty raccoons with masks in the shade,
Telling jokes that will never fade.

Badgers chuckle, rolling in grass,
As hedgehogs giggle while watching the pass.
A chorus of laughter fills up the air,
Beneath the leaves where joy's everywhere.

Revelations of Joy in the Thicket

Frogs croak tales with a twist of glee,
While fireflies blink like stars dancing free.
A plucky owl gives a wise, silly wink,
With stories so funny, they make you rethink.

Chipmunks exchange gossip, all in a row,
While bunnies hop, putting on quite a show.
In this raucous place, delight won't cease,
Nature's charm grants limitless peace.

Laughter in the Leafy Canopy

From above, the branches sway and sway,
Casting shadows where children play.
A woodpecker drums a merry beat,
As laughter echoes down to your feet.

The sun peeks through, a playful tease,
While butterflies swirl with delicate ease.
The leaves rustle secrets, a joyful sound,
In the canopy where fun knows no bound.

Whispers of Woodland Joy

A gentle breeze carries giggles so bright,
As gnomes share tales by the soft moonlight.
Each flower chuckles, each blade of grass,
Inviting all to let worries pass.

With foxes in masks and their playful ways,
They jive through the night, in a merry daze.
The forest hums with a joyful tune,
Under the gaze of the gleeful moon.

Nurtured by Nature's Nonsense

In the meadow, frogs wear hats,
Chasing butterflies, they dance like cats.
The trees giggle, leaves all a-twirl,
As squirrels plot mischief, oh what a whirl.

Beneath the sun, a rabbit hops,
In quirky shoes, he mischievously flops.
Chasing rainbows, who's here to play?
Nature's antics brighten the day.

Serenity in the Swaying Branches

The breeze whispers secrets, soft and sweet,
While dandelions tickle tiny feet.
A bird with an umbrella tries to fly,
As clouds in pajamas drift through the sky.

Flower crowns on ladybugs rest,
Each bloom a tale, nature's jest.
Awkward dances in the cool shade,
With laughter, the forest serenely swayed.

The Jester's Game in the Grove

Amid the trees, a clownfish danced,
With every splash, the flowers pranced.
Bubbles of laughter floated high,
As a snail wore glasses and winked an eye.

A raccoon juggles acorns, what a sight,
While owls hoot jokes, bringing delight.
Their woodland games, a merry tease,
In nature's court, they aim to please.

Wanders of Whimsy in the Wilderness

Twirling in circles, a ferret jumps,
While the brook giggles, bubbling with chumps.
A fox with a kite plays hide and seek,
In the whims of the wild, they're never meek.

The sun hides behind a ticklish tree,
As shadows dance like giddy glee.
With every twist, the stories unfold,
Of laughter and fun, in the wild, they behold.

Dance of the Dappled Light

In the woods where shadows play,
Sunbeams twirl like dancers gay,
Leaves rustle with a cheeky grin,
As laughter stirs the air within.

Squirrels chase their tails in flight,
Bouncing 'round with pure delight,
Nature's jesters, quick and spry,
Beneath the branches, they leap high.

Mushrooms giggle, sprightly crew,
Tickling toes with morning dew,
The brook chuckles, whispers tease,
With flutters on the gentle breeze.

In this realm where mirth abounds,
Each soft sound a joy resounds,
The dappled light, a playful tune,
Makes every heart a bright festoon.

Breezes of Blissful Laughter

A breeze sweeps through the grassy patch,
With every rustle, scents of hatch,
The daisies dance, a quirky sight,
As butterflies giggle in their flight.

Chasing shadows, the children run,
Poking fun, oh what a ton!
With every stumble, squeals arise,
Under the sun, in joyful guise.

The trees chuckle, swaying low,
As branches whisper secrets slow,
A world alive with funny sounds,
Where happiness and joy abounds.

Each tickling breeze a playful tease,
Bringing smiles with utmost ease,
In this wild, enchanted air,
Laughter bounces everywhere.

Chortles Under the Canopy

Underneath the leafy shade,
Chortles sparkle, never fade,
With each rustle, secrets fly,
Tickling ears as breezes sigh.

The bunnies hop in silly ways,
With twitching tails and playful plays,
While owls wink with sage advice,
Giggling softly, oh so nice.

Frogs croak rhymes, a quirky song,
Marshy friends all join along,
A symphony of chortles bright,
Underneath the silver light.

Nature's jesters, full of cheer,
In this realm, no room for fear,
With every wiggle, jump, and shout,
The giggles never, ever doubt.

The Secret Smiles of Nature

Among the leaves, a secret found,
Nature's smiles all around,
With each petal, bright and bold,
Whispers of laughter softly unfold.

The rabbits grin with mischief pure,
Plucking flowers for their lure,
While birds chirp witty little lines,
Making melodies like fine wines.

The brook chuckles as it flows,
Tickling pebbles, where joy grows,
With sunbeams bouncing on the stream,
Nature wraps us in a dream.

Every rustling in the glade,
Hints of humor are displayed,
In this land where spirits rise,
The secret smiles are nature's prize.

Bursts of Laughter in the Boughs

In the branches high and low,
Birds are chirping tunes of woe.
Squirrels dance and scamper fast,
Playing tricks, oh such a blast!

Leaves are rustling, secrets game,
Crickets join in with their name.
Beneath the shade, a fit of glee,
Echoes of joy, wild and free.

In the glade, the shadows leap,
While rabbit's antics wake from sleep.
Bouncing here and rolling wide,
Nature's laughter can't be denied!

Under canopies, fun is found,
With every silly, joyful sound.
From twig to vine, let smiles spread,
In this world, where dreams are fed.

Secrets of Springtime Whimsy

Breezes dance through fields anew,
Flowers laugh in every hue.
Bumblebees buzz with delight,
As daisies sway in the sunlight.

Frogs in ponds leap for a prize,
Each landing brings surprise and sighs.
Tadpoles frolic, not a care,
While butterflies spin in the air.

Sunrise paints the flirting skies,
With playful jests that often rise.
Chirps and chuckles fill the air,
The woods embracing joy to share.

Underneath this cheerful dome,
Creatures laugh, they feel at home.
Nature's stage, a grand parade,
In every shade, laughter's made.

The Playful Spirits of the Forest

Whispers echo through the trees,
A lively band, a breeze of tease.
Pixies peek from leafy beds,
With playful pranks, all laughter spreads.

Bouncing mushrooms, sing a song,
Where every note feels right and wrong.
Bunnies tumble, chase a whim,
As shadows dance on a forest limb.

The watchful owl, with eyes so wide,
Winks at antics he cannot hide.
In every nook and cranny bright,
Secrets bloom in sheer delight.

With mischief wrapped in nature's wrap,
The day is filled with giggles that clap.
Even the quiet stillness fights,
To join the fun on laughter's heights.

Ecstasy Among the Emerald Foliage

In the depths of verdant dreams,
Where nothing's ever what it seems.
Leaves chuckle, twirl on the ground,
As magic ebbs in laughter's sound.

In shady nooks, impish sprites,
Concocting jests on starry nights.
Twinkling fireflies join the show,
With winks and giggles, off they go.

Twirling vines and playful shouts,
Echo among all the leafy routes.
With every step, the world's aglow,
A sense of fun begins to flow.

Peeking through each emerald wall,
A merry chase, they heed the call.
In joyful leaps, both heart and mind,
A treasure of bliss, forever entwined.

The Cheerful Cadence of Nature

Beneath the broad and leafy roof,
Chirps and chuckles dance aloof.
A squirrel struts, a grin so wide,
His acorns rolled, he cannot hide.

The brook has secrets, whispers new,
It tickles rocks and dances, too.
A frog croaks loud, a comic show,
In this parade, all spirits glow.

Butterflies chase, a swirling flight,
Painting laughter through the light.
The flowers nod, they join the fun,
Beneath the smiling, golden sun.

Nature calls with a joyful sound,
Its melody spreads all around.
In this mirth, we feel alive,
Where every creature loves to thrive.

Serendipity in the Sylvan Shade

In shady groves where shadows play,
A chipmunk hides, then leaps away.
His friends all giggle, oh what fun,
As they chase rays of brightening sun.

The daisies sway in silly dance,
With bees that buzz and prance, romance.
A gentle breeze, a ticklish breeze,
Invites the trees to sway with ease.

Nearby a rabbit flops and tumbles,
His little feet make merry fumbles.
The chorus of laughter fills the air,
In woodland hideouts everywhere.

Beneath the bows, sweet serendipity,
Sprinkles joy with such simplicity.
A tapestry spun with happy threads,
In this green realm, where laughter spreads.

Festive Spirits Under the Palm

Beneath the palm, a party's begun,
With rustling fronds in the setting sun.
A parrot squawks with splendid flair,
As lizards join the lively air.

The sand crabs hop in tiny hops,
Their antics make the laughter pop.
They dance in circles, quick and spry,
While seagulls squawk and soar on high.

Palm leaves rustle, a quirky band,
Playing tunes, just as they planned.
With every note, the spirits rise,
In this festive spot 'neath sunny skies.

Oh, what a day for glee and play,
Where nature shows the brightest way.
Under the palms, we spin and sway,
Celebrating life in a merry ballet.

Harlequin Heights of the Woodland

In vibrant hues, the woods do gleam,
Where playful jesters chase a dream.
With nimble feet, they leap and prance,
In a woodland hide-and-seek romance.

The owls hoot, a raucous cheer,
While mischievous foxes draw near.
Their glances quick, a playful hunt,
In this theatre of woodland fun.

The sunbeams pierce through leaves' embrace,
As shadows dance in a merry chase.
Squirrels chatter, a funny refrain,
In this harlequin haven, joy remains.

From merry heights, the world below,
Is painted bright with laughter's glow.
As we tread softly through this space,
Mirth and magic find their place.

The Trysts of Tickle and Timber

In the glade where shadows sway,
Laughter dances in the day.
Squirrels wear their acorn hats,
Sharing jokes with chattering cats.

Frogs croak tales in silly tunes,
While owls sway beneath the moons.
Breezes blow with ticklish cheer,
Nature chuckles, bringing near.

Branches bend with playful spright,
Ticklish leaves take to flight.
A jolly game of hide and seek,
Echoes of laughter at their peak.

In the heart where joy resides,
Lively spirits, nature's guides.
With every creak and soft embrace,
A joyful meeting, a smiley face.

Joking with the Junipers

Beneath the boughs, the laughter flows,
Junipers giggle, as everyone knows.
A rabbit tells a pun so bright,
That even the wise old fox takes flight.

Twisting vines in a playful tease,
Tickled winds whisper through the trees.
Each rustle sparks a cheerful dance,
As critters frolic in a happy trance.

The moonlit night, a stage so grand,
With fireflies in their glowing band.
Every twig strummed with a tune,
Echoing laughter, beneath the moon.

When the sun peeks through the leaves,
Junipers chuckle, no room for grieves.
Nature's jesters, so full of cheer,
Invite all to join in, never fear!

The Festival of the Forest Folk

In a glen where no one frowns,
Forest folk wear their silly crowns.
Dancing round with glee and grace,
Swapping jokes in this woodland space.

Badgers rolling in the grass,
While the rabbits make a dash.
Squirrels juggle acorns high,
As flavors of laughter fill the sky.

The festival lights up the night,
Frogs croon songs that feel just right.
Moonbeams shimmer on every smile,
As all join in to laugh awhile.

With every cheer, the forest sways,
Filling hearts on these joyous days.
Through branches wide, the laughter flows,
In every nook, the fun just grows.

Pitter-Patter of Playful Whispers

A soft pitter-patter on woodland floor,
Whispers of fun knock upon the door.
Little critters with antics galore,
Create a song that we all adore.

Nimble feet dance in the glen,
With tiny tigers and gentle men.
Silly games that twist and twirl,
Nature's mischief in a happy whirl.

Leaves rustle, secrets shared in the breeze,
As mushrooms chuckle, bending their knees.
In shadows, shadows bounce with glee,
Weaving stories, wild and free.

Playful whispers weave through the night,
As stars above twinkle in delight.
With every giggle, joy takes flight,
In nature's heart, all is right.

Whimsy and Wonder in the Woods

In the forest, trees wear hats,
Squirrels dance on merry mats,
A rabbit juggles shiny stones,
While owls chuckle in their homes.

The brook sings songs of silly glee,
Trees sway, giggling tree to tree,
A deer trips over laughing ferns,
As sunlight into shadows turns.

Frogs in bow ties leap about,
Chasing butterflies with a shout,
While butterflies, in pastel hues,
Do a waltz in tiny shoes.

The woods are filled with light and cheer,
Every giggle close and near,
Nature's joy in every sound,
In this happy, playful ground.

Fancies of the Fern Fronds

Underneath the leafy shade,
Whimsical games are often played,
Ferns tickle toes, as they sway,
While ants march on in bright array.

Ladybugs in polka dots,
Share a laugh with tiny tots,
A woodpecker's silly knock,
Sends echoes 'round the rock.

Mice wearing hats of dandelion,
Chase each other, oh so fine,
They tumble, giggle, roll around,
In their fanciful playground.

Sunbeams catch a fairy's wing,
O'er blossoming flowers they sing,
The forest hums with pure delight,
From dawn till dusk, in joyful light.

Elfin Cackles in the Underbrush

In shadowed glens where mischief brews,
Elves paint the world in sparkly hues,
With twinkling eyes, they share a joke,
As mushrooms dance and clovers poke.

A hedgehog rolls, with laughter loud,
While daisies sway, all giggly and proud,
The critters join in merry play,
Brightening up the woods all day.

The crickets chirp in playful tune,
As fireflies dance beneath the moon,
A whimsical breeze whispers sweet,
Where forest friends and laughter meet.

In quiet corners, secrets bloom,
As nature's laughter fills the room,
A chorus of chuckles fills the air,
In the underbrush, without a care.

Lighthearted Lullabies in Leafy Nooks

Nestled in a cozy spot,
Stories told and laughter caught,
Breezes hum a gentle tune,
While shadows play beneath the moon.

Sleepy squirrels in a stacked pile,
Sharing dreams of cheeky style,
As crickets serenade the night,
With sleepy sighs and soft delights.

Hedgehogs snore on beds of moss,
Counting stars, their only gloss,
Fireflies blink like tiny lights,
Guiding dreams through starry nights.

In those nooks where laughter's heard,
Every rustle, every word,
In nature's arms, so warm and snug,
Embrace the joy, the silly hug.

Radiant Revelry Among the Roots

Under a tree where shadows dance,
A squirrel prances, taking a chance.
With acorns flying and laughter wide,
The woodland critters join the ride.

Chirps and chuckles fill the air,
As rabbits play without a care.
They hop and skip through sunlit beams,
Whispering secrets in merry dreams.

A turtle stumbles, trying to race,
Wobbling joyfully at an awkward pace.
The frogs croak tunes that waver and sway,
While bees buzz quickly, enjoying the play.

Daylight fades in a golden burst,
The evening hum turns into a thirst.
For laughter shared beneath the trees,
We find our hearts floating on the breeze.

The Cheer from Canopied Corners

In the corners where shadows blend,
A chorus of giggles begins to ascend.
The leaves are shaking with vibrant mirth,
As nature celebrates its wholesome birth.

Squirrels tease the sluggish deer,
With acrobatic stunts that draw near.
The chorus of joy is a sweet refrain,
Echoes of laughter dance in the rain.

A rabbit hops on a bouncing trail,
While the fox watches, trying to prevail.
The owls hoot with a wise old grin,
Encouraging the fun to begin again.

When dusk descends and stars ignite,
The antics continue until the night.
In canopied corners where giggles dwell,
Nature's revelry casts its spell.

Nature's Joyful Reverie

Amidst the greens where flowers prance,
The bumblebees join a merry dance.
Butterflies flutter with colors so bright,
Sprinkling joy with their delicate flight.

A hedgehog rolls into a ball,
Chasing its friends, oh what a haul!
The laughter rings out, crisp and clear,
Nature's delight, our hearts hold dear.

In a glen where wildflowers sway,
The sunbeams giggle as the children play.
Each whispering leaf and pittering paw,
Conspires to share in the joyous uproar.

As fireflies twinkle like stars from the ground,
The merriment fades with the night's gentle sound.
Yet in our hearts, we carry the light,
Of nature's humor, so pure and bright.

The Giggling Game of the Glades

In the glades where thick vines twine,
A game unfolds, both silly and fine.
With whispers and chuckles that echo around,
Adventure awaits on this playful ground.

Beneath the branches, shadows do flit,
As brush and bark join in the wit.
Each rustle and creak is a cue to respond,
For laughter is magic, of which we're all fond.

A parade of creatures, odd and spry,
Danced to the rhythm of a passerby.
They pranced and twirled in a lively spree,
Turning the glade into glee's jubilee.

When moonlight glows in a silver beam,
The game carries on, like a soft, sweet dream.
In the glades where the silly hearts race,
We find our joy, our little safe space.

Whimsy in the Whispering Woods

In the trees, a squirrel prances,
Chasing shadows, taking chances.
Frogs in hats play leap and bound,
Laughter echoes all around.

Winds sing soft and tease the leaves,
Chirping birds weave tales like thieves.
Mice with shoes dance quite the jig,
On a stage set by a twig.

Sunbeams waltz on dappled ground,
Every critter joins the sound.
Upside-down, a rabbit spins,
In this place, the fun begins.

With acorns tossed and laughter shared,
Each tiny creature's joy declared.
Here in woods where mirth does reign,
Playful hearts will never wane.

Flickers of Happiness in the Sunlight

Bumblebees buzz with gentle cheer,
Tickling blossoms, drawing near.
Ladybugs race on cotton blooms,
Joy awakens, dispels glooms.

Sunny patches, warm and bright,
Where ants march on in a line so tight.
Rabbits hop with silly glee,
Chasing shadows, wild and free.

The chatter of frogs—silly and loud,
As butterflies dance in a colorful crowd.
Every laugh that floats through air,
Makes the world a brighter lair.

Each playful heart, a joyful song,
Here, dear friends, you can't go wrong.
Embrace the warmth of fun in flight,
Sunlight flickers, spirits light.

Merriment on Mossy Paths

Beneath the pines, where shadows play,
Squirrels skitter, bright and fey.
Toadstools gather, round they sit,
Sharing tales, a perfect fit.

With giggly streams and dancing light,
Wobbly frogs leap with delight.
Every step on mossy ground,
Brings a chuckle, soft and round.

Breezes carry laughter's tune,
Tickling leaves like a cheerful June.
In this realm, where fun abounds,
Joy is lost, then quickly found.

Bouncing acorns, rolling leaves,
A place where whimsy never grieves.
Join the dance, come take a chance,
Let your spirit skip and prance!

The Lighthearted Lure of the Vale

In the vale where daisies bloom,
Laughter fills the open room.
Wobbling rabbits, full of cheer,
Share their secrets, drawing near.

Butterflies with painted wings,
Whisper tales of silly things.
In the warmth of sunny glades,
Teasing tales, a playful parade.

Chipmunks play a game of chase,
Scampering fast, keeping pace.
With each hop and silly yelp,
The vale giggles, no need for help.

So gather round and share the fun,
The lighthearted days have just begun.
Underneath the bright blue skies,
Joy abounds, and laughter flies.

The Elation of Earth's Embrace

In the meadow, shadows play,
Bunnies hop, and children sway.
Laughter bubbles like the stream,
Nature hums a joyful dream.

Ticklish leaves in the wind sway,
Squirrels scamper in a fray.
Jokes exchanged with rustling leaf,
The heart finds its silly relief.

Larks on a branch sing their tune,
While daisies giggle 'neath the moon.
A tickle of breeze, a wild chase,
Life's laughter, a warm embrace.

Sunbeams dance on faces bright,
In this realm of pure delight.
Here, joy's whispers roam free,
A merry place for you and me.

Enchanted Laughter in the Wild

Amidst the trees, a chorus sings,
Whimsical songs that joyfully cling.
A squirrel drops an acorn by,
And laughter echoes to the sky.

Breezes play peek-a-boo with leaves,
While sunbeams twirl with charming thieves.
The grass invites a game of tag,
With every step, a little brag.

Hiding fairies laugh and cheer,
As butterflies dance, no hint of fear.
Giggling flowers sway in delight,
As day turns softly into night.

In this enchanted, playful land,
The joy of nature, truly grand.
With hearts as light as clouds above,
We find sweet mirth and endless love.

Jovial Jests of the Timberland

In the woods, a trickster breeze,
Whispers jokes to swaying trees.
Mushrooms wear their happy hats,
As laughter rings from playful spats.

A bear mischievously steals a snack,
While birds dart, avoiding the pack.
The brook chuckles with each splash,
As critters dash in a cheerful flash.

Sunshine winks through leafy boughs,
While thyme and sage giggle with vows.
Stumps serve as thrones for giddy kings,
With the wild composing joyous flings.

Nature's stage a comical sight,
With friends who revel in pure delight.
Amidst the trees and whispers bold,
A joyful tapestry unfolds.

Lighthearted Larks Amidst the Green

In gardens lush, where laughter spills,
Breezes spin in quickening thrills.
Hummingbirds play a teasing game,
As blossoms blush and feel the same.

Swaying branches tell a tale,
Of fairies that are bound to sail.
Each flutter echoing a giggle,
While fawns skip sly and wriggle.

A playful fox with a feathered cap,
Leads the fun in a merry lap.
Joyful hearts dance, twirl, and prance,
In this green realm, they take a chance.

Underneath the sunlight's gaze,
Laughter rings in joyful ways.
In nature's arms, we find our cheer,
Creating memories we hold dear.

The Chorus of Hidden Mirth

In the shadows where sunlight bends,
A symphony of laughter blends.
Squirrels dance with acorn hats,
Chasing tails like playful chats.

The brook hums tunes of cheer and fun,
While flowers sway, their petals spun.
A bunny hops in comical glee,
Tickling toes of a nearby tree.

Mossy carpets where friends unite,
Crickets chirp through the night bright.
Their secrets shared in whispers low,
In this realm where chuckles flow.

Every rustle hides a silly jest,
Nature's jesters, they're at their best.
A wise old owl with knowing eyes,
Cracks jokes that make the whole world rise.

Frolics in the Forest Shade

Beneath the canopy so wide,
Little critters scurry and glide.
Here a rabbit, there a hare,
Playing tag without a care.

The sun peeks through in dappled rays,
Where shadows dance in playful ways.
A parade of ants with tiny drums,
Marching to their own funny hums.

Breezes whisper silly tunes,
Sending giggles up to the moons.
Treetops sway, a wobbly sight,
Filled with whispers of sheer delight.

With each rustle, there's a burst,
Of laughter quenching any thirst.
Here joy reigns beneath leafy spread,
Where all worries quietly shed.

Chuckles Among the Trees

Among the trunks with bark like smiles,
Wanderers share their playful styles.
A raccoon steals a shiny snack,
While a fox gives a cheeky quack.

Dancing leaves that twirl and spin,
Invite us all to join in.
The forest floor, a stage of fun,
Where shadows play and jokes are spun.

The old tree stump, a throne it seems,
Hosts giggling creatures' silly dreams.
Mushrooms giggle in their little caps,
As the world erupts in joyous claps.

With every twirl, a chuckle's heard,
In harmony without a word.
For in the woods, the spirit thrives,
Where happiness and humor jives.

Joyful Echoes of the Glade

In serene glades where laughter rings,
Playful creatures dance on wings.
A deer slips by with a silent leap,
Stirring whispers in dreams so deep.

Sunbeams tickle every face,
As nature holds a joyous space.
The echoes tease from nook to nook,
In every bush, a laughing brook.

Chirping birds join in the spree,
With silly tunes to set us free.
Hopping frogs join the loyal crew,
To share their songs from morning's dew.

With every rustle and soft sigh,
The spirit of cheer comes floating by.
Here in the glade, we find our bliss,
Where funny tales we can't dismiss.

The Frolicsome Heart of the Forest

In the shade where shadows prance,
Silly squirrels begin to dance.
Beneath the trees, they leap and twirl,
Spinning tales that make me whirl.

The brook gurgles with a teasing tone,
While playful whispers in breeze are blown.
Leaves poke fun in their rustling sound,
As creatures giggle all around.

A rabbit hops with a wiggly nose,
Chasing butterflies wherever it goes.
And all the flowers sway to a beat,
A merry band in this wild retreat.

Sunlight winks from the treetops high,
As shadows stretch to the sky.
Nature's laugh is a joyous song,
In this frolic, we all belong.

The Locket of Laughter in Leaves

Among the branches, magic sprinkles,
As leaves burst forth with secret twinkles.
A parrot shares a cheeky jest,
Creating laughter, none can rest.

In burrows deep, the critters plot,
With sneaky schemes that hit the spot.
A game of chase without a care,
As butterflies join, light as air.

The sun peeks out, a golden grin,
As mischief twirls like a capered spin.
Every branch tells tales of glee,
In the locket where joy runs free.

With every gust, a chuckle flies,
Tickling noses, sparking sighs.
Nature's laughter breaks the silence strong,
Embracing all who sing along.

Nature's Playful Vignette

In a meadow bright, the daisies play,
Waving their heads in a cheeky way.
A lazy bee starts to hum and buzz,
Rounding up friends for some joyful fuzz.

When clouds drift by like giant sheep,
Down below, the rabbits leap.
Each hop reveals a secret task,
In this wonderland, we need not ask.

A turtle grins with a wise old wink,
As the stream giggles, joining in sync.
Playful shadows dance on the ground,
While frolics and laughter abound.

The trees rustle with hearty cheer,
As the world spins on, far and near.
In nature's arms, where joy meets sight,
Every moment is pure delight.

Resplendent Revelations of the Woods

In the grove where wonders dwell,
The secrets of joy begin to swell.
A fox pokes fun at the sleepy deer,
While crickets chirp a concert clear.

Nestled high, a nest of glee,
With baby birds chirping carefree.
Their silly antics paint the day,
In hues of laughter on display.

A gentle breeze plays hide and seek,
Whispering secrets, soft and cheek.
The ferns sway with a wink of bliss,
Promising treasures one cannot miss.

As twilight paints the world in gold,
Nature's stories lovingly unfold.
With every rustle, a sweet surprise,
In the woods where laughter never dies.

Chortles in the Heart of the Glade

In the forest's playful cheer,
Frogs wear crowns and leap from here.
Squirrels dance on branches high,
As butterflies giggle by.

Breezes tickle every leaf,
Fluffy bunnies hold their grief.
Mushrooms wear their polka dots,
Telling jokes in tidy spots.

Hummingbirds buzz with delight,
While owls wink with feathered might.
Under trees where shadows play,
Laughter bubbles all the day.

Enchanted Smiles in Woodland Nooks

Squirrels natter with great glee,
Chasing dreams up every tree.
A hedgehog wears a tiny hat,
And winks as if he knows where's that.

Daisies dance in gentle rows,
While jolly breezes swirl and blow.
Each rustle of the leafy green,
Hides jokes that have not yet been seen.

Cardinals chuckle as they sing,
Swinging on a weathered swing.
In this nook, each thought's a game,
One can't help but feel the same.

The Merry Composition of Chirping Crickets

Crickets chirp a lively tune,
Underneath the shining moon.
Their laughter fills the night air bright,
While fireflies giggle, taking flight.

A rabbit hops with playful flair,
And tucks a dandelion in its hair.
Whispers weave through the tall grass,
As playful shadows come to pass.

Each note brings about a smile,
Nature's jesters all in style.
As the stars twinkle awake,
So do all the laughs we make.

Nature's Jests in Twilit Spaces

In twilight's glow, the woods awake,
Where shadows waltz and fairies shake.
A raccoon plays hide and seek,
With a soft giggle, oh so sleek.

The leaves rustle with quiet pranks,
While wet stones sit in merry ranks.
Each whispered breeze holds secrets dear,
Tickling ears that choose to hear.

Among the roots, in playful glee,
Toads croak rhymes, oh so free.
In this space where laughter thrives,
Nature's spirit truly strives.

Glee by the Glistening Stream

Laughter bubbles over, so bright and clear,
Banana peels slip, oh dear, oh dear!
Frogs in tuxedos, they waltz on a log,
With every leap, they dance like a frog.

Squirrels wear hats that are far too large,
Chasing their tails, they seem to discharge,
Peanut butter sandwiches float by in a line,
As giggles explode like bubbles of brine.

A turtle spins tales of his daring feat,
While a rabbit hops in shoes that fit neat.
The breeze plays along, makes the branches sway,
With funny little whispers that brighten the day.

Plenty of mischief, and joy galore,
In this playful realm, there's never a bore.
The sun beams down, setting hearts alight,
As laughter dances through day and night.

Euphoria of the Enchanted Glen

Fairies twirl high in the shimmering air,
Tickling the blooms, a laughter to share.
Bumblebees buzzing, they join in the fun,
Chasing their shadows beneath the warm sun.

A gnome with a grin stands guard by the stream,
Telling tall tales that make the trees beam.
With a wink and a nudge, he starts a good chase,
While flowers erupt in a jubilant race.

Crickets play music, a raucous affair,
A dance party starts, without a single care.
With giggles and snickers, they move to the beat,
As day gives way to an evening retreat.

Stars wink down softly, joining the jest,
Nature's own laughter, the absolute best.
In this magical place where joy freely flows,
Every chuckle lingers, and wonder just grows.

The Joyive Echo of Shadows

Under the branches, shadows prance and play,
Whispers of laughter float on their way.
A sneeze from a crow, such a playful surprise,
As owls roll their eyes and the night starts to rise.

Mice dance in slippers, tipped just so right,
While fireflies blink like stars in the night.
A gentle breeze carries a pun to your ear,
Where mischief unfolds and worries disappear.

The moon plays a tune, does a jig on the grass,
As jokers emerge in the shadows that pass.
Hidden behind trees, they snicker and spy,
Crafting more stories to share with a sigh.

Echoes of merriment bubble like streams,
Weaving together our most joyful dreams.
In this cheerful twilight, all frolic and groove,
As laughter dances lightly, a perpetual move.

Capering in the Quiet Grove

In the corner of woods where the bananas grow,
Dancing mushrooms giggle, putting on a show.
A hedgehog in glasses reads poetry aloud,
As laughter erupts, and the trees feel proud.

Breezes tell secrets of games long since played,
While rabbits declare a parade unafraid.
Pies made of clouds float in midair with grace,
Tickling the noses of all in this place.

Caterpillars chuckle, they wiggle and squirm,
While butterflies flutter, their colors confirm.
It's a raucous affair filled with joy and delight,
In the quiet of groves, everything feels right.

As day turns to dusk, the fun stretches on,
The stars blink in rhythm, a soft, twinkling song.
In the heart of the woods, where silliness reigns,
We caper and laugh through the soft refrains.

Frolic at Twilight's Edge

As the sun dips low, shadows dance,
Little critters play at a wild chance.
Whiskers twitching, tails in flight,
Squeaky whispers of delight.

Frogs in tuxedos leap and glide,
Chasing fireflies as friends confide.
The crickets chirp a silly tune,
To a mischief-making raccoon.

A squirrel juggles acorns with flair,
While birds exchange gossip without a care.
Laughter echoes beneath the trees,
As the breeze joins in with teasing tease.

At twilight's edge, hilarity reigns,
Nature's jesters break all the chains.
With every chuckle, the stars wink bright,
Wrapping the forest in pure delight.

The Hidden Humor of Nature's Grove

In the grove where the flowers sigh,
A snail races by, oh my, oh my!
With a wiggle and smile, it takes its run,
While ladybugs fret about missing the fun.

Bamboo giggles in the wind's embrace,
Each leaf a jester, every stem a face.
The rabbits snicker at a clumsy hare,
Tumbling over, but not a single care.

Mushrooms huddle, whispering jokes,
As butterflies tease the dancing folks.
A turtle pulls into its shell for fun,
While the shadows dance away with the sun.

In the grove, where joy takes its chance,
Nature's laughter is a carefree dance.
Every rustle, a chuckle, every sight,
The hidden humor brings sheer delight.

Breezes Carrying Melodic Murmurs

A playful breeze sweeps through the trees,
Whispering secrets to the buzzing bees.
They chuckle and buzz in perfect refrain,
As the dandelions laugh in the rain.

Squirrels play tag, up and down,
Chasing shadows all over town.
With each wiggle, leaf confetti flies,
Like sprightly laughter against the skies.

The bubbling brook joins in the fun,
Tickling rocks beneath the run.
Frogs puff up, claiming the stage,
As the forest erupts in a jovial rage.

With every murmur, a melody springs,
Nature's ensemble of playful things.
The world spins round in joyous glee,
Breezes carry laughter, wild and free.

Laughter's Footprints on the Forest Floor

Scattered giggles on the forest floor,
Little footprints lead to giggly lore.
A deer prances with a clumsy skip,
Joining in on the playful trip.

Over logs, through bushes, laughter bounces,
While a fox prinks, and the dandelion pounces.
Every twig crackles with a sly joke,
As the forest weaves tales of an old folk.

Hoots from owls, a wise crack or two,
Echo through the branches, fresh like dew.
The sun dips low, but joy won't hide,
With memories of chuckles as our guide.

Laughter echoes as shadows play,
Footprints of fun mark the day.
In the heart of the woods, let spirits soar,
For mirth in nature is what we adore.

The Glee of Celestial Canopies

Underneath a sky so wide,
The squirrels dance, they cannot hide.
With acorns flying, what a sight,
They twirl and spin in pure delight.

The sunbeams tickle leaves above,
While ants march on, a moving love.
Each twig a stage, each rock a throne,
In this domain, they're not alone.

The clouds bubble with joyful spark,
They whisper secrets in the park.
With every breeze, a playful cheer,
Nature laughs, we draw it near.

A chorus of chatter fills the air,
As laughter twirls without a care.
In canopies where fun takes flight,
Come join the giggles, feel the light.

Luminous Laughter Amidst the Pines

Beneath tall pines, the shadows play,
With jester winds that sway and sway.
The pinecones laugh, they tumble down,
And turn the frown of trees around.

Little critters in a chase,
With skittish steps, they find their place.
A tadpole leaps, a frog-like cheer,
In laughter's echo, joy is clear.

The moonlight sprinkles silver beams,
While owls wink as if in dreams.
A symphony of chirps and calls,
In this enchanted space, all enthralls.

With every rustle, giggles rise,
A merry tune beneath the skies.
Here in the boughs, with hearts so bright,
Laughter weaves through the moonlit night.

The Healthy Humor of the Horizon

In the morning glow, the laughter wakes,
As sleepy clouds do playful shakes.
The sun peeks out, a golden grin,
While streams join in with a bubbly spin.

The mountains chuckle, valleys hum,
As flowers bloom, they all succumb.
Nature's jesters wear crowns of green,
In this kingdom, laughter's seen.

Foxes frolic, and geese parade,
Every critter joins the charade.
While breezes whisper jokes so sly,
Under the arching, endless sky.

With every step, the joy expands,
In laughter's grasp, we hold its hands.
The horizon opens wide, so bright,
Promising fun in the morning light.

Delight in the Dappled Midnight

As candles of stars begin to glow,
The forest twitters, putting on a show.
With frolicsome shadows, a playful spree,
Midnight's charm brings glee like a spree.

A raccoon wearing a hat too wide,
Dances along with utmost pride.
With twinkling eyes, and mischief near,
In this nighttime kingdom, all is dear.

The whispers of breezes, like soft giggles,
Embrace the branches with subtle wiggles.
While fireflies blink, a starry jest,
In the dappled dark, they shine their best.

With laughter twinkling in every nook,
The midnight magic opens its book.
In this realm where fun ignites,
Delight blooms into the warmest nights.

Laughter Cascading Through Lilting Leaves

In the shade, where sunlight plays,
The children chase the fleeting rays.
With whispers soft and muffled squeals,
They spin about, like swirling wheels.

A squirrel steals a snack to munch,
The birds join in, not one to hunch.
A ticklish breeze begins to tease,
As laughter tumbles through the trees.

The daisies sway, their heads held high,
As giggles dance and spirits fly.
Their petals shimmer, bright and free,
In this realm of joy and glee.

They roll on grass, a mountain of mirth,
In this enchanted corner of Earth.
Each chuckle rings, pure and clear,
Resonating for all to hear.

The Merriest Moments in the Arboretum

Under branches, big and wide,
The kids take turns on a joyful ride.
They stumble, tumble, and fall with glee,
As laughter echoes through every tree.

A playful pup joins in the fun,
Chasing shadows, on the run.
With wagging tail and joyful yips,
He adds to the day's sweet antics and flips.

Clouds above begin to giggle,
As raindrops fall, they dance and wiggle.
But in the midst of every splash,
Laughter erupts, a happy crash!

With sticky hands and messy hair,
They share their sweets, with love to spare.
These moments glow, so bright, so warm,
Creating joy, like a cheerful storm.

Happy Harmonics in the Hollow

In a hollow, where shadows play,
Laughter bounces all around the day.
With silly songs and quirky rhymes,
They share their giggles, creating chimes.

A rabbit hops, with nimble feet,
Joining in, a playful treat.
With every jump and every cheer,
The laughter spreads, far and near.

Beneath the boughs, stories are spun,
Of frolics, fumbles, and endless fun.
Their spirits soar like birds in flight,
As friends unite, all day and night.

The leaves rustle, a rhythm sweet,
Carrying joy in a lilting beat.
In this haven, so carefree,
The heart learns what it means to be.

A Tapestry of Laughter in the Trees

Weaving tales under the leafy canopy,
A colorful mix, abundant as can be.
With each shared laugh, the world transforms,
Creating stories, in joyful swarms.

Silly antics, with jumps and shouts,
Echo, rise, and spin about.
Gathered friends, in circles tight,
Paint the air with delight and light.

A butterfly flits, attempting to join,
In a dance of mirth, so cleverly coy.
They spin around, lost in delight,
In this tapestry, heartstrings ignite.

Even twilight brings laughter's glow,
As stars twinkle, their secrets bestow.
With every chuckle, they find their way,
In this enchanted place, forever they'll play.

Frolic of the Forest Folk

In the glade where shadows prance,
Squirrels dance a merry dance.
With acorns tossed and laughter bold,
They spin their tales, both bright and gold.

Beneath the boughs, a rabbit lies,
Tickled by the buzzing flies.
He hops and giggles, quick as light,
Chasing beams that spark delight.

Frogs croak tunes, so offbeat sound,
While clumsy deer leap all around.
A raccoon's mask, a cheeky grin,
In the playful woods, all join in.

Whispers rise as breeze takes flight,
Beneath the stars, the woods ignite.
With each leap, each joyful cheer,
Nature's jesters, free and clear.

Serenade of Sunshine and Shadows

Sunshine tickles leafy shade,
Into the glen, the creatures parade.
A badger burrows, snorting cheer,
While spinning tales for all to hear.

With each flip and funny face,
The woodlands burst with playful grace.
A parrot squawks, a crafty word,
As laughter echoes, never heard.

The tiny ants march in a line,
Stumbling over twigs divine.
They trip and tumble, oh so spry,
In this sunlit show, they fly.

As twilight dims the brightened scene,
Laughter lingers, soft and keen.
Forests echo with jolly sound,
In the blend of shadows, joy is found.

The Delightful Mosaic of Meadow

In a meadow, bright and wide,
Butterflies like giggles glide.
A goat wears flowers in its crown,
With every leap, it twirls around.

Grasshoppers play tag in the grass,
Jumpy fellows, they zip and pass.
Each little leap, a funny cheer,
Bringing joy to all who hear.

The daisies nod, the breezes blow,
A rabbit sneezes with a show.
Frolic and laughter blend so sweet,
In this meadow, joy's complete.

As the sun dips, colors blend,
With schenanigans that never end.
The symphony of sounds composed,
Carried by winds, forever exposed.

Mirthful Moments in the Thicket

In the thicket, giggles hide,
Under leaves where critters bide.
The trees are whispering funny tales,
Of winding paths and playful gales.

A porcupine dons a silly hat,
While otters chase a wiggly rat.
The twinkle of eyes, a comical sight,
Filling the woods with pure delight.

Tails twirl and mischief stirs,
In this sanctuary, laughter purrs.
With every rustle, every sound,
Magic blooms within the ground.

As starlight drapes the thicket deep,
Creatures gather, it's time to leap.
With raucous joy, the moonlit spree,
In mirthful moments, wild and free.

The Woodland's Playful Reverie

In the glade where shadows dance,
Mushrooms wear their polka dots.
Squirrels spin in silly prance,
While rabbit stumbles, laughs a lot.

The breeze whispers jolly tales,
Of acorns rolling down the hill.
A chipmunk munching on some snails,
Chortles, causing quite the thrill.

Beneath the boughs, a puddle gleams,
Fairies leap with joyful grace.
Imagination's wild dreams,
Filling each soft, secret space.

A cacophony of quirks abound,
As crickets chirp their merry song.
Where joy and laughter will be found,
In this forest where we belong.

Frolicsome Fables of the Foliage

The oak tree tells its funny jokes,
While owls chuckle from their perch.
The underbrush is filled with pokes,
As playful leaves begin to lurch.

A hedgehog rolls and tumbles round,
His spiny coat becomes a ball.
With laughter echoing profound,
Nature's circus holds us all.

The daisies nod, their heads will sway,
To the rhythm of the playful breeze.
As woodland friends come out to play,
Creating mischief with such ease.

Beneath the sun's warm, gleaming rays,
The creek is bubbling, bubbling loud.
Where nature's music softly plays,
And laughter drapes like a bright shroud.

Smiles Painted in Soft Sunlight

Sunlight dapples on the ground,
Drawing smiles in patches bright.
Butterflies dance without a sound,
In a canvas kissed by light.

A lizard slips with a small cheer,
On a log that's warm and dry.
With every wobble, never fear,
He shines beneath the azure sky.

The flowers giggle in a breeze,
Winking at the buzzing bees.
A songbird croons with all its ease,
While squirrels munch and steal the keys.

In this woodland, laughter's fair,
With friends both furry, bright, and bold.
The joy walks lightly everywhere,
As sunshine on the heart unfolds.

Captured Giggles in Rustling Grasses

In the meadow, laughter springs,
From the tickle of the blades.
Bouncing, rolling, oh what flings,
Every critter's joy cascades.

The ladybugs play hide and seek,
As the grasshoppers jump high.
A gentle breeze will softly speak,
While the clouds float on by.

The ants are marching with a beat,
Each tiny footfall full of cheer.
Their minuscule, yet grand retreat,
Sparks hilarity, crystal clear.

The sun dips low, the shadows blend,
And whispers rise like puffs of air.
In every giggle, joys extend,
Nature's laughter everywhere.

Harmony in the Hushed Grove

In the grove where whispers dance,
Little critters take their chance.
Squirrels twirl with acorn hats,
While birds perform on tree branch mats.

Frogs leap high in silly jumps,
Joining in with all the chumps.
The wind carries giggles near,
Tickling leaves, spreading cheer.

Breezes swirl and spin about,
As flowers sway and laugh out loud.
The forest echoes with delight,
In harmony, a playful sight.

Each moment sparks a playful whim,
As shadows dance on nature's rim.
In laughter's hold, the day drifts by,
A symphony beneath the sky.

Mischief in the Sun-Dappled Thicket

Beneath the weave of branches bright,
Mischief brews in golden light.
A fox in socks chases a kite,
While rabbits leap in pure delight.

Butterflies join the game of chase,
Swirling in a vibrant race.
A sneaky crow stirs up some glee,
As sparrows giggle up in the tree.

The sunbeams laugh, a playful tease,
Twisting playfully in the breeze.
As nature's laughter echoes close,
Unveiling joy, a funny dose.

With every rustle, every cheer,
Adventures bloom, far and near.
In this glen of cheerful souls,
Mischief thrives, and joy unfolds.

Glee Adrift on a Gentle Breeze

Breezes float like feathers light,
Carrying tales of pure delight.
Whimsical winds whisper and tease,
Inviting laughter with each ease.

In dandelions, fairies sing,
Spinning stories on playful wing.
Caterpillars prance in line,
As rainbow colors intertwine.

Clouds chuckle, soft and round,
As smiles blossom from the ground.
Nature's joy, a sweet release,
In every rustle, every crease.

The world explodes in smiles today,
With every leaf, a child at play.
Adrift on breezes' tender touch,
Glee surrounds us, oh so much.

Tranquil Joy in the Green Embrace

In the heart of emerald trees,
Joy flutters by on gentle breeze.
A turtle hums a happy tune,
As crickets chirp beneath the moon.

Laughter flows from every nook,
As squirrels read from nature's book.
The branches sway with silly bends,
As playfulness in stillness blends.

Dewdrops giggle on morning leaves,
Spreading joy as day retrieves.
In quiet moments, magic blooms,
Disguised in worlds where laughter looms.

Together in this green embrace,
We find our smiles, our happy place.
With whispers soft and hearts so free,
Tranquil joy, our symphony.

Whimsy in the Whispering Willows

In the shade, with a chuckle and cheer,
Squirrels frolic, chasing who's near.
Leaves dance around, a jig so spry,
While shadows giggle as clouds drift by.

Breezes tease, like friends at play,
Tickling ears in a light-hearted way.
Nature's laughter in hues of green,
As playful sprites hop, oh what a scene!

Beneath the boughs, a riddle is spun,
Where laughter's the charm, and joy's never done.
With every rustle, a new joke unfolds,
In this woodland realm, adventure beholds.

A picnic laid out, with pies piled high,
Ants in a line, they march and comply.
"Will you share?" a voice asks with glee,
In a world so bright, there's room for all, you see.

Delightful Banter Among the Ferns

Ferns sway lightly, a green rolling tide,
Whispers of laughter where secrets abide.
A caterpillar grins with googly eyes,
While butterflies twirl in colorful skies.

In this lush nook, where shadows convene,
A turtle contemplates, yet still looks keen.
"Did you hear the one about the old snail?
He dreamed he'd fly, but just left a trail!"

Frogs croak back with sarcasm so bright,
"Your joke's a stretch, but I'll take flight tonight!"
They leap and they splash, a chorus of fun,
As nature's humor shines bright like the sun.

The brook's babble joins in on the wit,
As rocks chuckle softly at every little bit.
Laughter erupts in a joyous refrain,
Among the ferns, where comedy reigns.

Revelry in the Roots

Beneath the trees, a party takes flight,
Roots intertwine, a marvelous sight.
A rabbit cracks jokes, so clever and spry,
As badger nods softly, with a glint in his eye.

Crickets sing songs, a jovial score,
While owls chuckle from high up, encore!
"Who's the wise one?" a young chipmunk jests,
"Not me," says the owl, "but I laugh with zest!"

Squirrels debate who can leap the most grand,
While mushrooms giggle, lending a hand.
With every pun shared, the forest ignites,
Beneath the roots, where the humor excites.

As dusk settles in with a soft twinkling star,
The laughter carries, it travels so far.
In this merry land, no gloom shall prevail,
For joy blooms eternal in each print and trail.

Amusement Under the Arching Boughs

Boughs open wide in a green, leafy hall,
Where laughter echoes, inviting us all.
A hedgehog spins tales of mischief and fun,
While the raccoons dance, their hoots weigh a ton!

Under branches, a feast laid with care,
Fruit is the punchline; oh, wouldn't we share?
"Whose turn is it to tell the next tale?"
As giggles erupt, we never grow stale.

The woodpecker taps to set up the beat,
While green ants parade on their tiny, quick feet.
"Let's tell of adventures in hollows and nooks,
Of treasure and laughter and mischievous looks!"

And as twilight deepens, with stars all aglow,
The jests take a turn, and the spirits all flow.
In merriment wrapped in the night's soft embrace,
We find joy in together, this magical place.

The Playful Dance of Forest Spirits

In meadows bright, where shadows leap,
The sprites in skirts begin to creep.
They twirl and spin, a merry sight,
In laughter's hold, from day to night.

With rustling leaves, they form a band,
Tickling trees with tiny hands.
A chuckle here, a giggle there,
As sunlight winks through leafy hair.

The brook joins in, with ripples wide,
A splash of joy, they cannot hide.
With every bounce, a song takes flight,
In playful dance, all hearts feel light.

So listen close, to nature's cheer,
Where spirits play and bring good cheer.
In every rustle, laugh, and prance,
The forest breathes its jolly dance.

Mirth in the Mossy Hollow

In a hollow deep, where whispers hum,
Chubby squirrels play, oh, what a sum!
They leap and tumble, they roll and flop,
With every misstep, they never stop.

The mushrooms giggle, as fairies play,
Beneath the ferns, they laugh all day.
While crickets chirp their silly tunes,
Beneath the watchful, smiling moons.

A rabbit slips, with ears askew,
The laughter bubbles, it's all so true.
In this hollow, joys intertwine,
Every chuckle, a sweet design.

So if you wander where moss does grow,
And hear the laughter of friends aglow,
Just know the magic in this space,
Brings smiles to every hidden face.

Reviving the Color of Laughter

Colors pop in the sunlit court,
Where bright flowers dance, a lively sport.
The butterflies ride on comical trails,
Telling tales of stumbles and fails.

The honeybees hum their joyous song,
As they buzz around, where they belong.
With each bloom's sway, laughter takes flight,
Painting the air with sheer delight.

The turtles crack jokes from their logs,
Making the snails laugh, along with frogs.
A canvas of joy painted so bright,
Reviving the hues of pure delight.

So join the scene in vibrant hues,
Where every chuckle is a welcomed muse.
In nature's palette, find your way,
To laughter's light, come out and play!

Serenade of Swaying Branches

Branches sway in a dancing line,
Tickled by winds that feel divine.
They whisper secrets, oh-so-keen,
In tunes of laughter, bright and green.

The owls hoot jokes from the nearby pines,
While soft sunlight in the forest shines.
With every sway, the world goes round,
As laughter echoes through the ground.

Dandling leaves, they shake and jive,
Inviting all to come alive.
The world's a stage for every critter,
In nature's band, no one's a quitter.

So listen close when you hear the breeze,
It carries giggles among the trees.
In this serenade of swaying cheer,
Find all that sparks joy, bring it near.

Crescendos of Cheerful Chimes

In a meadow of winks and soft sighs,
The laughter of children lights up the skies.
Each tickle of breeze, a playful delight,
Chiming joyously in morning's bright light.

Jumps in the grass where the daisies sway,
Skipping around as the sun holds sway.
With butterflies twirling in rhythmic embrace,
A chorus of giggles fills up the space.

The trees sway along with the whimsical sound,
While shadows of gigglers flit all around.
Each moment a jest, in the soft afternoon,
Their mirth dances gently, a fanciful tune.

In the glow of the eve, the warmth lingers near,
Echoes of laughter we hold so dear.
As twilight descends, hearts still aglow,
In symphonies cheerful, the good vibes will flow.

A Ballet of Blossoms and Laughter

Among petals that twirl on a soft, gentle breeze,
Dance little sprites, as they play among trees.
Each blossom a dancer, with joy they prance,
In the heart of the garden, they whirl and they chance.

With a splash of bright colors, the tulips take flight,
And the daisies respond with a giggle of light.
Mirth woven through petals, laughter takes cue,
Sprinkling the air like freshly bloomed dew.

In the ballet of blooms, the laughter runs free,
As shadows chuckle softly, we join in with glee.
Round and around in this nature-born stage,
We twirl through the laughter, the joy, and the age.

With each twinkle and giggle, the evening grows sweet,
The blossoms embrace us, the night feels complete.
In a world full of wonder, we gather anew,
In a ballet of laughter, where dreams toss and brew.

Happiness Wrapped in Greenery

On a blanket of green, we chuckle and roll,
Wrapped in the warmth of a playful stroll.
The leaves whisper secrets, the grass has a grin,
In the heart of the forest, our laughter begins.

With a hop and a skip, we dance through the glade,
Where the sunlight dapples, the shadows invade.
Tickles from blossoms and sweet crafty breezes,
In the bounty of nature, our joy never ceases.

The squirrels lend an ear, with their eyes all aglow,
As we spin our wild stories, with a frolicsome flow.
In this emerald wonder, we're free as can be,
Wrapped up in happiness, just you and me.

The whispers of laughter, the rustle of leaves,
A symphony crafted where imagination weaves.
Encircled by green, we revel and play,
In this blissful embrace, let our cares drift away.

Larks in Lush Retreats

In the heart of the thicket, the larks take wing,
A melody of laughter, in chorus they sing.
Bouncing on branches, they soar with delight,
In the lush, leafy hideouts, all is so bright.

With each playful chirp, the giggles resound,
As flowers erupt all around on the ground.
In the giggling breeze, we join in their song,
Larks laughing with us, where we all belong.

Beneath leafy canopies, joys intertwine,
As we weave through the ferns, sweet moments align.
The sun dips low, casting shadows so kind,
In this lush retreat, all our worries unwind.

As night cloaks the glade, our spirits take flight,
Guided by laughter, we dance into night.
In the soft, whispered calls, we find our sweet peace,
In the laughter of larks, our joys never cease.

www.ingramcontent.com/pod-product-compliance
Lightning Source LLC
Chambersburg PA
CBHW072148200426
43209CB00051B/841